W£alth

IMELDA RODRÍGUEZ

BOOK SERIES BY FIG FACTOR MEDIA

WordPower Book Series

© Copyright 2023, Fig Factor Media, LLC.
All rights reserved.

All rights reserved. No portion of this book may be reproduced by mechanical, photographic or electronic process, nor may it be stored in a retrieval system, transmitted in any form or otherwise be copied for public use or private use without written permission of the copyright owner.

It is sold with the understanding that the publisher and the individual authors are not engaged in the rendering of psychological, legal, accounting or other professional advice. The content and views in each chapter are the sole expression and opinion of its author and not necessarily the views of Fig Factor Media, LLC.

For more information, contact:

Fig Factor Media, LLC | www.figfactormedia.com

Cover Design & Layout by Juan Pablo Ruiz
Printed in the United States of America

ISBN: 978-1-959989-51-6
Library of Congress Control Number: 2023915604

DEDICATION

To God be the Glory! To my beautiful daughter, who fills my life with happiness. You are my biggest inspiration. To my mother, who always believed in me.

ACKNOWLEDGMENTS

First and foremost, praise and thanks to the God, the Almighty for his showers of blessings to complete this coffee table book successfully. I would like to express my deep and sincere gratitude to Jackie Camacho Ruiz for giving me the opportunity to leave a legacy for future generations.

Thank you, Izar Olivares, for the stunning work to walk with me side by side in this process. Fig Factor Media Publishing has been my one and only publisher and I am pleased with the results. I truly appreciate the support to make this happen.

Of course, to my mother because you take care of Valeria Zoe while I write to bring this to life.

INTRO

Generational wealth has been resonating with me for such a long time. I chose the word WEALTH because many people can see it as a dream or even something impossible to reach. I became a Financial Coach back in 2014, two years after working for two shelters in the city of Chicago. Those two years taught me about homelessness, but I learned that the only thing to do is to get out of that stage as fast as possible. I felt that there was something else I could do to help people prevent it, so I transitioned to homeless prevention. There, I fell in love with Financial Coaching. Now I was able to help my community with the steps to take before getting close to moving into a shelter.

As a Financial Coach there are lots of things I can do with my clients: dreaming, planning, understanding, strategizing, creating—just to name a few. Everything that can help them see things out of their box. The possibilities are endless. This is one of my favorite parts of coaching—the action plan. Here is where the gear of dreaming turns into a reality. I remember one of my clients who was part of the shelter for domestic violence, she was dreaming about having her own home at one point. It took her seven years to go from homelessness to homeownership. Stories like hers are the ones that fuel my tank to keep moving forward. I have been seeing my clients reach their goals and that is the beauty of it.

IN THE BEGINNING

According to the Guinness World Records, the best-selling book of all time is the Bible. Research conducted by the British and Foreign Bible Society in 2021 suggests that the total number probably lies between 5 to 7 billion copies. In the 21st century, Bibles are printed at a rate of around 80 million per year.

Saying that, I am using the Bible as reference to see what it says about Wealth. Personally, I don't like or believe in religions, but I do believe in having a constant and regular relationship with the creator of ALL things. I am a reader and every time I read a book there is always something that comes from the Bible. Throughout this book there will be verses to reflect on. Keep in mind that 2350 verses are related to finances in the Bible.

"In the beginning God created the heavens and the earth."
(Genesis 1, NIV)

www.Guinessworldrecords.com

WELL-BEING

"Honor the Lord with your wealth, with the first fruits of all your crops; then your barns will be filled to overflowing, and your vats will brim over with new wine." (Proverbs 3:9-10, NIV)

God does not need my money, but when I give with honor to the one that gave me first I am understanding that everything I have is because of him. The job, the business, the contract, the client, the income is coming to me because He allows it to happen.

There is a big difference between giving and giving with honor. I can give anything to anyone, but when I give with honor I do take my time, resources, and efforts to choose the best. Every time I give to God, He keeps taking care of me.

THE BLESSING

"The blessing of the Lord brings wealth, without painful toil for it." (Proverbs 10:22, NIV)

As a financial coach, I have provided one-on-one and group financial coaching sessions since 2014. During this time, I have had the opportunity to meet with individuals, couples, and groups from different cultures, races, languages, backgrounds, incomes, credit scores, immigration status, social/economic status, etc. I have the privilege of working with homeless to very wealthy individuals/couples/groups. We all are different when we deal with money for many reasons. Poor or rich, money is not an easy task to manage.

Today, there is pressure to buy more than what we can afford. Messages are coming our way for us to have more and to buy more. For the same reason people want to get money faster—doing anything at any cost. Just remember that money that comes with sorrow won't bring you joy. His blessings will always bring you joy, do not give up on your faith.

LEAVING A LEGACY

"A good person leaves an inheritance for their children's children, but a sinner's wealth is stored up for the righteous." (Proverbs 13:22, NIV)

During my financial coaching journey, it is very common for clients to worry about their current financial situation versus their future. I would say about 2% or less come to me to talk about inheritance. This number could be higher if clients are not living day to day. Around 64% of Americans are living paycheck to paycheck, according to a May 2022 survey. As a result, 64% are not going to leave any legacy for their own children, nor for their children's children.

What could you do today to leave a legacy? If you are not leaving an inheritance, the very least you can do is to pay for life insurance. If you do not have it yet, get one as soon as possible so you do not leave them any more problems. Go Fund Me is not fun at all.

Life insurance will be something similar to leaving your loved ones with a (fishing) net that will support them while they adjust their new life without you. I am pretty sure they have dreams and a life that needs to continue with or without you. The best time to get life insurance is right now.

How Many Americans Are Living Paycheck to Paycheck? | Credit Cards | U.S. News (usnews.com)

SHARING IS CARING

"The generous will themselves be blessed, for they share their food with the poor." (Proverbs 22:9, NIV)

As a mom, one of the hardest things to teach a child, let alone an only child, is to share. Yes, there are books, videos, classes, real experiences, and many more things that support these efforts, but it is still not an easy task. We are not born knowing how to share. Sadly, many grown-ups still work with that social and moral value.

I am teaching my six year old daughter to share by allowing her to see me share meals with the less fortunate. Once a month, as a family we volunteer our time with a food program from our local church. Actions weigh more than just saying it. We the parents/grandparents/caregivers/teachers carry the responsibility to teach the future generations and we need to do whatever it takes to teach them to share with others. As a result, we can expect better neighborhoods, schools, churchs, business, communities, cities, states and nations. Saying that, whatever you are doing to teach kids and young generations will impact the world exponentially.

TRUST IN THE LORD

"But blessed is the one who trusts in the Lord, whose confidence is in him." (Jeremiah 17:7-8, NIV)

Back in March 2020, the Covid-19 pandemic impacted many of us. It has not been easy to recover from the economic effects during that time. I am not sure when everything will go back to where it used to be, or if it can. One thing has been clear to me, my trust is in Him; He will take care of me and my own.

I have not had a day without a meal, which I am thankful for. Things are not easy and not coming to my door just for trusting. I have been working and looking for contracts and partnership for my businesses, but the combination of work while trusting in the Lord has been key to opening important doors. We all have difficult situations, some financials and some others not but I challenge you to trust in the Lord and to increase your faith.

TREASURES IN HEAVEN

"Do not store up for yourselves treasures on earth, where moths and vermin destroy, and where thieves break in and steal. But store up for yourselves treasures in heaven, where moths and vermin do not destroy, and where thieves do not break in and steal. For where your treasure is, there your heart will be also." (Matthew 6:19-21, NIV)

I grew up in a prominent family, my mother inherited a legacy. My grandmother passed without a will, and my mother, being the oldest, was responsible for splitting everything. As her heart was not interested in the treasure, she split it equally. Sadly, my uncle was always fighting to have more and that brought tension to my family. Years passed, he tirelessly kept pushing to have more and more until my mom could not handle it anymore, so she decided to move out of that toxic environment by selling her land and building so she physically could be out of the equation.

Now ask yourself, where is my treasure? Is that treasure bringing any tension to me or my family?. Do not allow for any treasure to come between you and your loved ones. No treasure on earth is worth it if your heart is part of it. The things that you cannot see have more worth than gold. I encourage you to write a list of your own cannot see-inventory.

Cannot see inventory: A list of the things you cannot see but that you possess.

GIVING COMES FROM YOUR HEART

"Give, and it will be given to you. A good measure, pressed down, shaken together and running over, will be poured into your lap. For with the measure you use, it will be measured to you." (Luke 6:38, NIV)

I am an only child and, believe me, I grew up having every necessity covered, but at the same time I remember myself always sharing and giving from what I have. I heard that when you have siblings you will be a person that can give easily. In my own experience, I can tell you it is not about having siblings or being an only child. To give comes directly from your heart. We get rich when we give, including your resources and/or your time.

"In this world it is not what we take up, but what we give up, that makes us rich." - **Henry Ward Beecher**

YOUR OWN HOUSEHOLD

"Anyone who does not provide for their relatives, and especially for their own household, has denied the faith and is worse than an unbeliever." (1 Timothy 5:8, NIV)

There are many people who want to change the world and who aspire to do big things. The question is: What are they doing already for their own household? Does their home have everything they need? Not just the basic needs but, are all their needs covered including love? Are you giving them the time they need? Do you know each other? Is there anything they need that you are not seeing?

One thing I know about Mother Teresa is that she was a person who read the bible. She once said, "If you want to change the world, go home and love your family." This is a very simple way to say what the apostle Paul wrote in the book of Timothy. Make sure to provide for your own household.

GOD WILL NEVER FORSAKE YOU

"Keep your lives free from the love of money and be content with what you have, because God has said, 'Never will I leave you; never will I forsake you.'" (Hebrews 13:5, NIV)

Money is an amazing tool and there is nothing wrong with having money and with wanting more than what we have now. The tricky part is when we cross that fine line to become miserliness.

I have had the privilege of working with many non for profits for years, and I can tell you that there are always people with money giving their money to those in need to support the mission of some or many organizations working in the communities. Those funders and foundations know and understand the principle of generosity, every time they sow a seed that seed will bring more fruit to their barns than anything else.

The opportunity I had working those two years in those shelters: Men in Crisis and Families in Crisis gave me the opportunity to understand all the ways a person can be pleased or content with what they have at that moment.

- Express gratitude for everything you have now (not tomorrow, now).
- Do what you love
- Enjoy simple things
- Meditate (read your bible and pray)
- Live in the present
- Forgive yourself
- Forgive others
- Show people you appreciate them

And to this list, I will add a very important point to the top of the list. Always remember that God will never leave you or forsake you.

ALWAYS OWE LOVE TO EACH OTHER

"Love Fulfills the Law. Let no debt remain outstanding, except the continuing debt to love one another, for whoever loves others has fulfilled the law." (Romans 13:8, NIV)

Debt alone is not a nightmare, but what makes things harder for someone to dream big and to keep moving forward are the outstanding debts. When you borrow, you become a slave to the lender. This applies to any amount, not just the big amounts. It is extremely important for you to pay your bills and to pay them on time.

The best debt we can all have in our records is the one to love one another. As the Bible description of love said, "Love is patient, love is kind. It does not envy, it does not boast, it is not proud. It does not dishonor others, it is not self-seeking, it is not easily angered, it keeps no record of wrongs. Love does not delight in evil but rejoices with the truth. It always protects, always trusts, always hopes, always perseveres. Love never fails." (1 Corinthians 13:4-8, NIV)

YOUR FATHER IN HEAVEN KNOWS THAT YOU NEED ALL THESE THINGS

"Therefore I tell you, do not worry about your life, what you will eat or drink; or about your body, what you will wear. Is not life more than food, and the body more than clothes? Look at the birds of the air; they do not sow or reap or store away in barns, and yet your heavenly Father feeds them. Are you not much more valuable than they? Can any one of you by worrying add a single hour to your life?" (Matthew 6:25-27, NIV)

Stress and anxiety are more common than ever, those have been part of our regular life. Not just in adults but in kids as well. Covid-19 increased the financial stress to many families and individuals in the whole world. If you are struggling with your finances, you do not have to solve it alone. Reduce the stress and anxiety by talking with a Financial Coach as this can help you increase your financial well-being. Us Coaches can help you see things that you are not seeing as we are out of your box.

If you are a head of household, I can tell you that kids and/or family members can feel your stress and they become stressed as well and believe me nothing good can come out when stress and anxiety are present. Every time you feel worried about something bring those worries to God, do what you need to do and remember that He knows your needs. Trust more and worry less. The best is yet to come!!

ABOUT THE AUTHOR

Imelda Rodriguez is the founder and CEO of Coaching Vida, LLC. She created the company to provide the necessary tools to obtain a better lifestyle through holding seminars, courses, workshops, and conferences, as well as one-on-one and group coaching sessions (life and financial coaching) that she named Coaching Vida LLC.

She is also the founder and author of Latinas in Finances, a book-movement that was launched in January 2023. Changing the financial narrative one Latina at a time, the book is a collaboration of women that share their personal stories of success and falls within finance. Imelda was also a contributing author for Today's Inspired Latina, Vol. III.

She is founder of the Entre Nosotras Talk Show, a video blog that has been live for more than ten years revolving around women's supporting topics. Imelda is also a Credit as Asset Master Trainer, among many other certifications that support her work. In June 2021, she received the Latina Community Spirit Award from the Latinas Voice Awards.

Throughout her work, Imelda has remained committed to multigenerational legacy. She deeply believes that we can be the best version of ourselves and we can grow and develop our greater purpose and impact through learning. The best is yet to come!

CONTACT:
hello@latinasinfinances.com | CoachingVida21@gmail.com
(312) 912-3222 | (312) 694-5364
Facebook: @LatinasinFinances
Instagram: Latinas.in.Finances
LinkedIn: @latinas-in-finances
latinasinfinances.com

HOW DOES THE WORD **WEALTH** EMPOWER YOU?